Beyond Heaven: The Christian Journey After Death

Christian A. Dickinson

Title: *Beyond Heaven*
Subtitle: *The Christian Journey After Death*
Written by: Christian A. Dickinson

Illustrations by: Learning Engineered LLC
Published by: Learning Engineered Publishing

Library of Congress Control Number: 2025945938
ISBN (Print paperback): 978-1-965741-47-4

First Edition: 2025

Printed & Created in: United States of America
Text and Illustration Copyright © 2025

Learning Engineered Publishing is a division of Learning Engineered LLC and a subsidiary of Carpe Diem Unlimited Holdings, Inc.

LEARNING ENGINEERED
PUBLISHING

Dedication

To Caleb, Amelia, Abigayle, Darcy, and Mitchell—may Jesus' light lead you through every adventure, from this life to the next, with hearts full of hope.

Preface

G rowing up, my home was a warm haven where elderly relatives and missionaries on sabbatical often stayed. Their voices echoed a truth that shaped my heart: *"To be absent from the body is to be present with Christ"* (2 Corinthians 5:8). That promise became a lighthouse, guiding me through life without fear of death. I saw death not as an end but as a doorway to Jesus, God's Son, who offers eternal life through His sacrifice. As a child, this belief made death feel safe—like stepping into a room already filled with love.

As I grew older, I discovered a darker side. Some preachers used the afterlife as a scare tactic—warning about separation from God in ways that drove people to faith out of fear rather than love. I met people who became Christians not because they longed for Jesus, but because they wanted to avoid "the other place." Faith, for them, felt like dodging a storm.

Over time, I learned that logic can lead you to faith's doorstep, but it is awe—the breathtaking wonder of God's love—that draws you into true devotion. I've written about that awe elsewhere, capturing moments when God's glory felt like a sunrise breaking open my soul.

Yet even among Christians, I noticed a troubling reality: many still fear death. Their fear wasn't rooted in doubt of God but in uncertainty about what comes next. Over the years, friends, neighbors, and strangers alike have shared their unease, shaped by vague images of fluffy clouds, glowing angels, or an afterlife that didn't make sense.

I believe the Bible offers something far clearer and more hopeful: a step-by-step journey that replaces dread with purpose. Scripture teaches that life on earth is preparation—learning to love and follow Jesus—and His plan for eternity is like a map through unfamiliar territory. That's why I wrote *Beyond Heaven: The Christian Journey After Death*—first for my children, and also for anyone searching for the truth about what lies beyond the grave. My prayer is that it clears away confusion about "heaven" and replaces fear with God's promise of love.

Christians may hold different views about the afterlife—on the timing of Christ's return or the nature of eternity—but this book reflects one biblical perspective, rooted in a literal reading of Scripture, particularly Revelation. Whatever your background, I hope this journey will stir your curiosity, strengthen your faith, and deepen your trust in God's loving plan.

Introduction: A Clear Path Beyond Death

Death is a question that tugs at every heart. What happens when we take our last breath? Many people picture "heaven" as a single, blurry place—fluffy clouds, golden gates, or a glowing afterlife where everyone ends up. But this confusion, as I've heard from countless people, turns death into something scary. They wonder, "What's 'heaven' really like? Is it even real?" The Bible, the sacred book Christians follow, offers a different picture: a clear, step-by-step journey after death, like a road trip with five distinct stops, not a foggy maze. I wrote *Beyond Heaven: The Christian Journey After Death* for my kids, grandkids and anyone seeking truth, to clear up misconceptions about "heaven," replace fear with hope, and share God's plan for what comes next. You don't need a Bible or prior knowledge—just an open mind and a curious heart.

The fear of death often comes from the unknown, mixed-up ideas blending paradise, a divine city, or eternal life into one vague "heaven." But the Bible's plan is like a map with clear signs, guiding us through what Christians believe happens after death. Through Emma, a Christian who trusts Jesus, God's Son, we'll follow this journey from the moment her soul—her inner spark, like the part that loves and dreams—leaves her body to her final place with God. Jesus, who Christians believe died to offer everyone a chance at eternal life, guides Emma through each step, turning fear into awe. This isn't the "heaven" of movies or fairy tales—it's a specific plan, grounded in God's love, that promises joy for those who trust Him.

This book unfolds in five simple chapters, each with the Bible's own words so you can see God's promises clearly:

- **Chapter 1: After Death: Paradise or Hades** shows where Emma's soul goes first—not "heaven" as most think, but a joyful rest or a sad place, based on faith in Jesus.

- **Chapter 2: The Second Coming and Resurrection** reveals Jesus returning to give Emma a new, forever body, proving death isn't the end.

- **Chapter 3: The Millennial Reign** follows Emma reigning with Jesus in a glorious city for 1,000 years, a time of peace, not vague "heaven."

- **Chapter 4: Satan's Release and Defeat** shows evil crushed forever, proving God's power over fear.

- **Chapter 5: The Great White Throne Judgment** leads Emma to eternal life, not a generic "heaven," through her faith.

Each chapter answers questions like: Where do we go first? What happens to our body? What's eternity like? By including every key Bible verse, I've made sure you can follow along without searching elsewhere. For my kids, I wanted a book that makes death clear and hopeful, not scary. For you—whether you're a Christian, a parent, or just curious—this book invites you to explore what Christians believe about the afterlife. It's a journey of awe, not fear, showing death as a step toward God's love. Imagine knowing death is a doorway to joy, not darkness—what would that change for you? As you read, let Emma's story guide you to reflect on your own hopes and questions about eternity.

Acknowledgements

Nick Vasiliades

Robert G. "Coach" Neff

Michael Duggar "MD", Esquire

Dr. Angela Everett

Contents

1

After Death: Paradise or Hades

E mma, a devoted Christian, closes her eyes in death, but her story doesn't end.

Christians believe the soul—your inner self, like the part that feels joy, dreams, and loves—lives on after the body dies. The Bible, the book guiding Christian faith, teaches that when you die, your soul goes somewhere right away, based on whether you trusted Jesus, God's Son, who Christians believe offers salvation through His death and resurrection.

For those like Emma, who love and follow Jesus, that place is paradise, a realm of joy and rest in God's presence, not the vague "heaven" people often imagine. For those who reject God, it's Hades, a temporary place of sadness and separation from Him.

This first step in the Christian journey after death is like stepping off a plane at a rest stop, not the final destination. It shows death isn't a scary void but a doorway to God's plan, easing fear with hope and awe for believers.

Emma's faith in Jesus leads her to paradise, where she feels a warmth like sunlight on a perfect day, her fears of death melting away like morning mist.

The Bible confirms this immediate transition in Luke 23:43 (English Standard Version):

> *And he said to him, "Truly, I say to you, today you will be with me in paradise."*

Jesus spoke these words to a man dying beside Him on a cross, promising that believers enter paradise right after death.

For Emma, paradise isn't the "heaven" of fluffy clouds or golden harps—it's a real place where she's wrapped in God's love, free from pain or worry. Her soul rests in peace, surrounded by a light that feels like Jesus' embrace, and the fear she once heard others express about death is gone.

Christians believe the soul, created by God to live forever, carries your essence—your thoughts, feelings, and love—into eternity, as shown in Genesis 2:7 (English Standard Version):

> *then the Lord God formed the man of dust from the ground and breathed into his nostrils the breath of life, and the man became a living creature.*

Just as God gave life to the first human, He welcomes Emma's soul to paradise, a place of awe and joy.

The Bible contrasts paradise with Hades through a story Jesus told about two men with different lives and destinies.

> Luke 16:19-31 (English Standard Version):
> *There was a rich man who was clothed in purple and fine linen and who feasted sumptuously every day. And at his gate was laid a poor man named Lazarus, covered with sores, who desired to be fed with what fell from the rich man's table. Moreover, even the dogs came and licked his sores. The poor man died and was carried by the angels to Abraham's side. The rich man also died and was buried, and in Hades, being in torment, he lifted up his eyes and saw Abraham far off and Lazarus at his side. And he called out, 'Father Abraham, have mercy on me, and send Lazarus to dip the end of his finger in water and cool my tongue, for I am in anguish in this flame.' But Abraham said, 'Child, remember that you in your lifetime received your good things, and Lazarus in like manner bad things; but now he is comforted here, and you are in anguish. And besides all this, between us and you a great chasm has been fixed, in order that those who would pass from here to you may not be able, and none may cross from there to us.' And he said, 'Then I beg you, father, to send him to*

my father's house—for I have five brothers—so that he may warn them, lest they also come into this place of torment.' But Abraham said, 'They have Moses and the Prophets; let them hear them.' And he said, 'No, father Abraham, but if someone goes to them from the dead, they will repent.' He said to him, 'If they do not hear Moses and the Prophets, neither will they be convinced if someone should rise from the dead.'

This story shows Lazarus, who trusted God, resting in paradise (called Abraham's side), a place of comfort and joy. The rich man, who rejected God, suffers in Hades, a temporary place of anguish separated from paradise by an uncrossable divide.

For Emma, this confirms her faith leads to peace, not fear, as her soul basks in God's presence.

Christians believe this step—paradise for believers or Hades for those who reject God—is temporary, like a waiting room before the next parts of God's plan.

Emma's joy in paradise is like arriving at a cozy inn after a long trip, knowing the journey continues.

Hades, though, is a place of regret for those who turned away from Jesus' offer of salvation, which Christians believe is a gift of love, as John 3:16 (English Standard Version) says:

For God so loved the world, that he gave his only Son, that whoever believes in him should not perish but have eternal life.

Unlike the blurry "heaven" of popular culture, paradise is a specific stop, not the final eternity, offering believers like Emma assurance and awe. This clarity transforms death from a frightening mystery into a defined step in God's plan.

For my kids, I want them to know death isn't something to fear but a moment to trust Jesus, who lights the way.

For you, this step invites reflection: What would it feel like to know death leads to a place of peace, not darkness?

As Emma rests in paradise, her journey is just beginning, filled with the awe of God's love and the promise of more to come.

2

The Second Coming and Resurrection

E mma rests in paradise, her soul wrapped in God's peace, but her journey is far from over.

Christians believe death is a step toward a glorious moment called the Second Coming, when Jesus, God's Son, returns to earth in power and glory to gather His followers. For Emma and other Christians who have died, this moment brings resurrection—their souls receive new, eternal bodies that are perfect and never wear out.

Living Christians at that time are transformed instantly, joining Jesus in the air in an event called the rapture. This second step in the Christian journey after death is like getting a new, unbreakable car for an endless adventure, proving death isn't the end but a doorway to new life. It's not the vague "heaven" people imagine but a specific, awe-inspiring moment in God's kingdom, replacing fear of death's finality with hope and wonder for believers.

As Emma waits in paradise, she hears a sound like no other—a commanding shout, an archangel's voice, and a trumpet blast that echoes like a victory call.

The Bible describes this moment in 1 Thessalonians 4:16-17 (English Standard Version):

> *For the Lord himself will descend from heaven with a cry of command, with the voice of an archangel, and with the sound of the trumpet of God. And the dead in Christ will rise first. Then we who are alive, who are left, will be caught up together with them in the clouds to meet the Lord in the air, and so we will always be with the Lord.*

This passage shows Jesus returning with divine authority, like a king arriving in triumph.

Emma, one of the "dead in Christ," feels her soul unite with a new body, rising from paradise to meet Jesus in the air. Her heart races with awe as she sees Him, His glory shining like a radiant dawn.

Living Christians, transformed in an instant, join her in this rapturous moment, their bodies made new without dying. The fear of death Emma once heard others express is gone, replaced by joy and wonder, knowing she's forever with Jesus, the One she trusted in life.

The Bible explains the nature of Emma's new body, which is far greater than her earthly one.

1 Corinthians 15:42-44 (English Standard Version):

> *So is it with the resurrection of the dead. What is sown is perishable; what is raised is imperishable. It is sown in dishonor; it is raised in glory. It is sown in weakness; it is raised in power. It is sown a natural body; it is raised a spiritual body. If there is a natural body, there is also a spiritual body.*

Emma's resurrected body is imperishable—it can't get sick, grow old, or die. It's raised in glory, glowing with God's light, like a star in a clear sky. It's raised in power, strong like a superhero, far beyond her frail earthly body.

This "spiritual body" isn't a ghost but a perfected physical form, designed for eternal life with God, as real as the first human God created in Genesis 2:7 (English Standard Version):

> *then the Lord God formed the man of dust from the ground and breathed into his nostrils the breath of life, and the man became a living creature.*

Just as God formed Adam from dust, He recreates Emma's body, no matter how she died—whether buried, cremated, or lost—because His power knows no limits.

Jesus promised this reunion in John 14:3 (English Standard Version):

> *And if I go and prepare a place for you, I will come again and will take you to myself, that where I am you may be also.*

This promise fills Emma with awe, knowing she's forever with Jesus.

This resurrection isn't the "heaven" of popular imagination—a cloudy, eternal rest—but a specific step toward God's eternal kingdom.

For my kids, I want them to know death doesn't end life but leads to a new, forever body, like upgrading to a perfect version of themselves.

For you, this step shows death's power is broken, replacing fear with hope. Christians believe all believers, whether long dead like Emma or alive at Jesus' return, are united in this moment of awe, their new bodies ready for God's next plan.

What would it feel like to know death leads to a new, unbreakable life?

As Emma rises, her heart full of joy, she knows her journey is leading to even greater wonders in God's kingdom.

Summary: Christians believe that when Jesus returns at the Second Coming, those who died trusting Him, like Emma, are resurrected with new, eternal bodies, and living believers are transformed to join Him, replacing fear of death with hope and awe.

3

The Millennial Reign

Emma, now in her radiant, resurrected body, stands with Jesus in the New Jerusalem, a city glowing like a sunrise with God's glory.

Christians believe this marks the millennial reign, a 1,000-year period when Jesus rules the earth with His resurrected followers, including Emma, while Satan, the rebellious angel who opposes God, is bound and unable to deceive.

This third step in the Christian journey after death is like a peaceful kingdom after a stormy battle, not the vague "heaven" people imagine. It shows God's plan to restore the world, filling Emma with awe and replacing fear of chaos with hope for believers, especially kids who might worry about evil's power.

Emma's heart swells as she serves in the New Jerusalem, a city radiant with God's presence, like a home filled with light.

The Bible details this era in Revelation 20:1-6 (English Standard Version):

> Then I saw an angel coming down from heaven, holding in his hand the key to the bottomless pit and a great chain. He seized the dragon, that ancient serpent, who is the devil and Satan, and bound him for a thousand years, and threw him into the pit, and shut it and sealed it over him, so that he might not deceive the nations any longer, until the thousand years were ended. After that he must be released for a little while. Then I saw thrones, and seated on them were those to whom the authority to judge was committed. Also I saw the souls of those who had been beheaded for the testimony of Jesus and for the word of God, and those who had not worshiped the beast or its image and had not received its mark on their foreheads or their hands. They came to life and reigned with Christ for a thousand years. The rest of the dead did not come to life until the thousand years were ended. This is the first resurrection. Blessed and holy is the one who shares in the first resurrection! Over such the second death has no power, but they will be priests of God and of Christ, and they will reign with him for a thousand years.

Emma, part of this first resurrection, serves as a priest and ruler, sharing Jesus' authority in the New Jerusalem, described in Revelation 21:2 (English Standard Version):

> *And I saw the holy city, new Jerusalem, coming down out of heaven from God, prepared as a bride adorned for her husband.*

Her role fills her with awe, knowing she's part of God's plan, and any fear of chaos she heard others express is gone.

While Emma reigns, the earth below is transformed into a place of peace, like a garden blooming after a drought.

Mortal people—descendants of those who survived earlier events—live long lives, build homes, and raise families under Jesus' perfect rule.

The Bible describes this in Isaiah 65:20-21 (English Standard Version):

> *No more shall there be in it an infant who lives but a few days, or an old man who does not fill out his days, for the young man shall die a hundred years old, and the sinner a hundred years old shall be accursed. They shall build houses and inhabit them; they shall plant vineyards and eat their fruit.*

Even nature reflects this harmony, as Isaiah 11:6-9 (English Standard Version) says:

> The wolf shall dwell with the lamb, and the leopard shall lie down with the young goat, and the calf and the lion and the fattened calf together; and a little child shall lead them. The cow and the bear shall graze; their young shall lie down together; and the lion shall eat straw like the ox. The nursing child shall play over the hole of the cobra, and the weaned child shall put his hand on the adder's den. They shall not hurt or destroy in all my holy mountain; for the earth shall be full of the knowledge of the Lord as the waters cover the sea.

This vision of animals and children living without fear shows a world filled with God's love, easing Emma's heart and proving evil has no power during this time.

This millennial reign, distinct from the "heaven" of popular culture, is a foretaste of eternity, where Emma serves with purpose.

Christians believe some mortals follow Jesus during this time, while others don't, setting the stage for future events.

For my kids, I want them to know this peaceful kingdom shows God's love wins, so they don't fear the world's chaos.

For you, this step offers comfort: death leads to a role in God's plan, not an uncertain end.

What would it feel like to live in a world where peace reigns and fear is gone?

As Emma serves in the New Jerusalem, her journey continues toward an even greater eternity, filled with awe at God's glory.

Summary: Christians believe that during the millennial reign, resurrected believers like Emma rule with Jesus in the New Jerusalem while Satan is bound, and the earth enjoys peace, replacing fear with hope and awe.

4

Satan's Release and Defeat

E mma reigns with Jesus in the New Jerusalem, a city shining like a beacon with God's glory, during a 1,000-year period of peace.

Christians believe this millennial reign, with Satan bound, is a time of harmony, like a calm harbor after a storm. But the Bible teaches this isn't the end.

In this fourth step of the Christian journey after death, Satan, the rebellious angel who opposes God, is released briefly, stirring trouble among mortal people on earth. He deceives some into a rebellion led by nations called Gog and Magog, but God crushes it with fire from heaven, casting Satan into the lake of fire forever.

This step, like a storm stopped by a mighty shield, proves God's power over evil, not the vague "heaven" people imagine. It fills Emma with awe and replaces fear of chaos with hope, especially for kids who might worry about bad things winning.

Emma watches from the New Jerusalem, her heart steady as God's justice unfolds.

The Bible describes this moment in Revelation 20:7-10 (English Standard Version):

> *And when the thousand years are ended, Satan will be released from his prison and will come out to deceive the nations that are at the four corners of the earth, Gog and Magog, to gather them for battle; their number is like the sand of the sea. And they marched up over the broad plain of the earth and surrounded the camp of the saints and the beloved city, but fire came down from heaven and consumed them, and the devil who had deceived them was thrown into the lake of fire and sulfur where the beast and the false prophet were, and they will be tormented day and night forever and ever.*

Satan, freed after 1,000 years, deceives some mortals—descendants of those living under Jesus' rule—into a vast rebellion, symbolized as Gog and Magog, names from ancient prophecies (Ezekiel 38–39).

They surround the New Jerusalem, where Emma serves, their numbers like a sea of sand. But God's response is swift: fire from heaven consumes the rebels instantly, like a lightning bolt ending a storm.

Satan is then cast into the lake of fire, a place of eternal judgment, distinct from the temporary Hades or the "hell" often confused with "heaven" in popular culture. Emma feels awe at God's power, her heart free from the fear of evil others have shared with her.

This event shows that even in a perfect world, some mortals choose to reject Jesus, unlike Emma, whose faith keeps her secure.

The lake of fire, where Satan joins other defeated evil forces, is a final boundary, not a place believers like Emma will ever see.

Christians believe this victory clears the way for God's final judgment, where all souls face their eternal destiny.

For my kids, I want them to know evil can't win against God's love, so they don't fear chaos.

For you, this step offers comfort: death leads to a future where God's power triumphs, filling believers with hope.

What would it mean to know that no evil can stand against God's plan?

As Emma stands firm in the New Jerusalem, her journey moves toward its final, awe-inspiring step.

Summary: Christians believe that after 1,000 years, Satan is released, deceives some mortals into rebellion, and is defeated by God's fire, cast into the lake of fire forever, replacing fear with hope and awe.

5

The Great White Throne Judgment

E mma, having witnessed Satan's defeat, stands before the final step in God's plan: the Great White Throne Judgment.

Christians believe that after the millennial reign, every soul—from paradise, like Emma, or Hades, and all who have died—faces God's judgment. This moment, like a final test where faith in Jesus is the answer, determines eternal life or eternal separation, not the vague "heaven" people imagine.

Emma's faith leads to joy, filling her with awe and replacing fear of judgment with hope, a message I want my kids to hold onto so they face the future with confidence.

Emma stands before a throne glowing with God's authority, her heart full of peace.

The Bible details this judgment in Revelation 20:11-15 (English Standard Version):

Then I saw a great white throne and him who was seated on it. From his presence earth and sky fled away, and no place was found for them. And I saw the dead, great and small, standing before the throne, and books were opened. Then another book was opened, which is the book of life. And the dead were judged by what was written in the books, according to what they had done. And the sea gave up the dead who were in it, Death and Hades gave up the dead who were in them, and they were judged, each one of them, according to what they had done. Then Death and Hades were thrown into the lake of fire. This is the second death, the lake of fire. And if anyone's name was not found written in the book of life, he was thrown into the lake of fire.

This passage shows a throne so majestic that creation itself steps back. The "books" record every deed, but the Book of Life holds the names of those who trusted Jesus, like Emma, whose faith secured her place in paradise and the first resurrection.

Christians believe salvation through faith, not just good deeds, writes your name in this book, as John 3:16 (English Standard Version) says:

For God so loved the world, that he gave his only Son, that whoever believes in him should not perish but have eternal life.

Emma stands confidently, her name in the Book of Life, feeling awe, not fear. Those whose names are absent face the lake of fire, eternal separation from God, distinct from the temporary Hades. The casting of Death and Hades into the lake of fire means death and suffering end forever for believers, a victory Emma shares.

The Bible emphasizes Jesus' universal authority in Philippians 2:10-11 (English Standard Version):

so that at the name of Jesus every knee should bow, in heaven and on earth and under the earth, and every tongue confess that Jesus Christ is Lord, to the glory of God the Father.

Every soul, from paradise or Hades, acknowledges Jesus as Lord, fulfilling God's plan.

For Emma, who trusted Jesus in life, this moment is a joyful affirmation, like a child running to a loving parent. She bows willingly, her heart overflowing with awe, entering eternal life—a state of unending joy, not the generic "heaven" of popular culture.

Christians believe those who rejected Jesus, like Paul before his conversion, bow when they see His glory as the

Light of the World, as in Acts 9:3-6 (English Standard Version):

> *Now as he went on his way, he approached Damascus, and suddenly a light from heaven shone around him. And falling to the ground, he heard a voice saying to him, "Saul, Saul, why are you persecuting me?" And he said, "Who are you, Lord?" And he said, "I am Jesus, whom you are persecuting. But rise and enter the city, and you will be told what you must do."*

Paul, once an unbeliever, was overwhelmed by Jesus' radiant truth, compelling him to bow and change. At the judgment, unbelievers see this same light, bowing involuntarily as the truth dawns too late, leading to the second death, eternal separation from God.

Yet, Jesus' offer of salvation, open to all in life, fills Emma with hope, not fear, showing judgment is a gateway to joy for believers.

For my kids, I want them to know faith in Jesus means facing judgment with confidence, like passing a test with the right answer.

For you, this step invites reflection: What would it feel like to stand before God with awe, not fear, knowing your name is in His book?

Summary: Christians believe that at the Great White Throne Judgment, believers like Emma enter eternal life through faith, while those not in the Book of Life face eternal separation, replacing fear with hope and awe.

6

Conclusion: Emma's Journey and the Christian Hope

Emma's journey through death to eternal life is like a map through a land of mysteries, offering clarity where others see only fog.

Christians believe this five-step path—paradise or Hades, resurrection, millennial reign, Satan's defeat, and final judgment—replaces confusion about "heaven" with truth and fear with awe.

I wrote this book for my kids and anyone seeking truth, to show that death isn't a scary end but a doorway to God's love, guided by Jesus, who Christians believe offers salvation to all who trust Him. Emma's story, rooted in the Bible's promises, brings hope to those who fear the unknown, turning death into a journey of wonder.

Let's walk through Emma's path to see how it brings clarity and comfort.

In Chapter 1, Emma's soul entered paradise, a place of joy with God, not the "heaven" people imagine, as Jesus promised in Luke 23:43:

> *"Truly, I say to you, today you will be with me in paradise."*

Unlike Hades, where those who reject God wait in sadness (Luke 16:19-31), paradise showed Emma that death is a beginning, easing fear with peace. This step reflects my childhood belief:

> *"To be absent from the body is to be present with Christ."* —2 Corinthians 5:8

This truth kept death from being scary.

In Chapter 2, Jesus returned at the Second Coming, giving Emma a new, eternal body, like a superhero version of herself (1 Thessalonians 4:16-17; 1 Corinthians 15:42-44).

This resurrection proved death's defeat, filling her with awe and banishing fear of finality, as Jesus promised in John 14:3:

> *"And if I go and prepare a place for you, I will come again and will take you to myself, that where I am you may be also."*

Chapter 3 brought Emma to the New Jerusalem, reigning with Jesus for 1,000 years in a peaceful world, not "heaven" but God's kingdom (Revelation 20:1-6; Revelation 21:2; Isaiah 65:20-21, 11:6-9).

This era showed God's love restores creation, easing fear of chaos.

In Chapter 4, Satan's brief rebellion was crushed, and he was cast into the lake of fire, proving evil's powerlessness (Revelation 20:7-10).

Finally, in Chapter 5, Emma faced the Great White Throne Judgment, her faith securing eternal life, not a vague "heaven" (Revelation 20:11-15).

She bowed joyfully to Jesus, while unbelievers, overwhelmed by His glory like Paul was (Acts 9:3-6), bowed too late (Philippians 2:10-11). Yet, Jesus' offer of salvation, open to all in life, shines with hope:

> *"For God so loved the world, that he gave his only Son, that whoever believes in him should not perish but have eternal life."* —John 3:16

This timeline reflects God's justice and mercy, a balance Christians believe defines His plan.

Emma's journey shows believers move from death to eternal life, filled with awe at God's love, not fear of the unknown. The Bible's clarity—unlike the blurry "heaven" of clouds and harps—offers a roadmap for eternity.

For my kids, I want them to know death is a step toward joy, not something to fear, because Jesus lights the way.

For you, this journey invites reflection: What does it mean to know death leads to God's presence? Does it ease your fears?

Christians believe Jesus' offer of salvation is a gift of love, open to all who choose Him in life, turning judgment into a moment of hope. Whether you're a Christian, a parent teaching your kids, or someone curious, Emma's story shows death as a path to awe, not dread.

What would it feel like to face eternity with confidence, knowing God's love guides you?

As Emma stands in eternal life, her journey calls you to consider the hope and wonder of God's plan.

Summary: Emma's journey through five biblical steps clarifies "heaven," replaces fear with awe and hope, and invites all to reflect on Jesus' offer of salvation.

7

The Afterlife Adventure: A Gamer's Guide to Eternity

Yo, gamer squad! Picture the Christian journey after death as the ultimate open-world RPG with five epic levels to God's victory. You're the hero, Jesus is your guide, dropping loot and wisdom. Let's grind!

Level 1: The Respawn Hub (Paradise or Hades)

Spawn Point: Death | XP: Faith points | Loot: Eternal hope Health bar zero? Your soul spawns in Paradise with Jesus—a glowing hub of God's love, unlocking only with His invite (Luke 23:43). No faith? Hades is a lonely map far from God's light, with zero XP (Luke 16:19-31). Pick wisely!

Level 2: Epic Power-Up (Second Coming & Resurrection)

Trigger: Jesus returns | XP: Glorious body | Loot: Immortal stats

Jesus drops a Roblox-style cutscene—trumpets, angels, hype! You get a glitch-free avatar for eternity (1 Thessalonians 4:16-17).
Pro Tip: Score the "Immortal Buff"!

Level 3: Co-Op Kingdom (Millennial Reign)

Map: New Jerusalem | Duration: 1,000 years | Buffs: Peace, guidance
Team up with Jesus in a flawless server—Satan banned (Revelation 20:1-6). Mortals build lives, but some risk a solo run later (Revelation 20:7-8).
Easter Egg: New Jerusalem shines as God's HQ!

Level 4: Final Boss Battle (Satan's Release & Defeat)

Boss: Satan + Gog & Magog | God's Move: Holy fire
Satan's Fortnite-style rush ends with God's fire—Game Over! He's banned to the Lake of Fire (Revelation 20:7-10).
Achievement: "Evil Defeated."

Level 5: Victory Screen (Great White Throne Judgment)

Checkpoint: God's Throne | XP: Eternal life | Loot: Infinite joy
Gamertags in the Book of Life unlock a boundless Minecraft world (Revelation 20:11-15). Unbelievers face the second death.

Easter Egg: Every player bows to Jesus (Philippians 2:10-11).

Quest Complete: Faith is the ultimate strategy guide. Emma's journey shows how to win—start yours, Darcy and friends! Check the Glossary for epic terms!

8

Christian's Questions After Writing This Book

Hey, my awesome kids, or any curious reader—writing *Beyond Heaven* helped me unpack God's plan for what happens after we die, but some things still feel like a cliffhanger. And that's okay! God's got the full map, and we'll see it one day. Here are a few questions I had while writing, so you can explore them too and feel the same hope I did.

If God is so loving, why would he create such a terrible place like hell?

Hell is a hard topic, but here's the truth: God's love is so big it gives us freedom to choose Him—or not. From the start, in Eden, He designed life as a relationship with Him (Genesis 2:8). Where God is, there's love, peace, joy, light, and belonging (Galatians 5:22).

But love isn't real if it's forced. Lucifer rejected God's love and chose pride instead (Revelation 12:4). Many people do the same. And because God respects our choice, He created a place for those who don't want Him. That place is hell.

Hell isn't God being cruel—it's God honoring the decision of people who say, "I don't want You." And if God isn't there, then everything opposite of Him takes over: instead of love, there's hate; instead of peace, despair; instead of joy, anger; instead of light, only darkness (Matthew 25:41,46).

God doesn't want anyone to end up there (2 Peter 3:9). That's why He sent Jesus—to rescue us and give us eternal life with Him (John 3:16).

Hell exists because God won't force His love.
Heaven exists because He longs to share it with us forever.
The choice is ours.

What's life like for mortals during the 1,000-year reign?
In Chapter 3, we saw Jesus ruling from the New Jerusalem, with Satan locked up and the world peaceful, like a fresh Eden (Revelation 20:1-6). Mortals—people who didn't get raptured—live long lives, build homes, and raise families (Isaiah 65:20-21). Even lions and lambs hang out together (Isaiah 11:6-9)!

But what about the everyday stuff? The Bible doesn't go into much detail. I like to imagine a calm world where Jesus' love shines everywhere, and mortals can still choose to follow Him. Some may rebel later (Revelation 20:7-8), which sounds wild, but it shows God's justice.

Is the New Jerusalem on Earth, and can mortals see it?
The Bible says the city comes down from heaven, glowing like a divine fortress (Revelation 21:2). It's the home base for resurrected believers like Emma (Revelation 20:4-6). Mortals might catch glimpses of it—a constant reminder of Jesus' rule—but they don't live there.

Could it exist in God's eternal time (Kairos) rather than our everyday clock time (Chronos)? Maybe! That's part of the mystery, and it's okay not to have all the answers.

Why the gaps in the story?
God gives us the big picture: paradise, new bodies, ruling with Jesus, evil defeated, and eternal life (John 3:16). The blurry parts—like the exact details of mortals' lives—aren't missing; they're reserved for later. That's not scary—it's epic!

I wrote this for you so you can feel awe, not worry, about eternity. Trusting Jesus is like grabbing a golden ticket to this incredible adventure. What's that mean for you? Let's keep seeking Him together!

9

Glossary

The following terms, used in *Beyond Heaven: The Christian Journey After Death*, are explained to help you, your kids, or anyone new to the Bible understand Emma's journey. Each definition uses simple language, like a guide for a new adventure, so the afterlife feels clear and hopeful.

- **Book of Life**: A divine record, like a guest list for eternity, holding the names of those who trust Jesus, ensuring joy at judgment (Revelation 20:12-15).

- **Eternal Life**: Living forever with God, like a never-ending party filled with love, for those who trust Jesus, not the vague "heaven" people imagine (John 3:16).

- **First Resurrection**: When believers like Emma get new, forever bodies at Jesus' return, like upgrading to a superhero body that never breaks (Revelation 20:5-6).

- **Gog and Magog**: Names for nations deceived by

Satan, like a team that loses a big game, showing some reject God even in a perfect world (Revelation 20:8).

- **Great White Throne Judgment**: The final moment when God judges all souls, like a test where faith in Jesus is the answer, leading to eternal life or separation (Revelation 20:11-15).

- **Hades**: A temporary place of sadness for those who reject God, like a gloomy waiting room, not "hell" or "heaven" (Luke 16:19-31).

- **Lake of Fire**: Eternal separation from God for those not in the Book of Life, like a final boundary, distinct from Hades (Revelation 20:14-15).

- **Millennial Reign**: A 1,000-year period when Jesus rules with believers, like a peaceful kingdom where everyone gets along, not "heaven" (Revelation 20:1-6).

- **New Jerusalem**: A glorious city where Emma reigns with Jesus, like God's beautiful home on earth, not "heaven" (Revelation 21:2).

- **Paradise**: A joyful rest with God after death, like a happy rest stop with Jesus, not the final "heaven" (Luke 23:43).

- **Rapture**: When living believers join Jesus in the air, like a big family reunion, easing fear of death (1 Thessalonians 4:17).

- **Resurrection**: New, eternal bodies for believers, like getting a perfect, unbreakable version of yourself (1 Corinthians 15:42-44).

- **Salvation**: God's gift of eternal life through faith in Jesus, like a key to a joyful forever, open to all who choose Him (John 3:16).

- **Second Coming**: Jesus' return to gather believers, like a hero coming back to save his friends, easing fear (1 Thessalonians 4:16-17).

- **Second Death**: Eternal separation in the lake of fire for those who reject Jesus, unlike believers' joy, a serious choice (Revelation 20:14-15).

- **Soul**: Your inner self, like your heart, thoughts, and dreams, living forever after your body dies (Genesis 2:7; Luke 16:19-31).

A Parent's Guide to Teaching the Afterlife

Dear Parents,

Beyond Heaven was written to help kids see death not as something to fear, but as a hopeful step into God's love. As a parent, you may sometimes feel unsure about how to explain the afterlife—especially if these truths are new to you. This guide is here to support you with simple ways to share Emma's journey, sparking faith-filled conversations that encourage both hope and curiosity. Whether you're reading with children or teens, you can make the afterlife an adventure of trust and joy.

Tips for Talking About Death

For Younger Kids (Ages 8–12):

Keep the focus on God's love and paradise as a happy, safe place with Jesus (Luke 23:43). If questions about Hades or the lake of fire arise, gently explain that Jesus offers salvation as a free gift (John 3:16). Use simple words like: *"God wants us with Him forever, and Jesus shows us the way."*

For Teens (Ages 13–18):
Encourage them to ask big questions about eternity and why some people choose not to follow Jesus. Connect the story to their world—for example, compare the "respawn hub" in the gaming guide to paradise. Be honest when mysteries remain (like in "Christian's Questions"), reminding them that we can trust God with the answers.

For All Ages:
Share your own faith journey. If you've ever struggled with fear of death, tell your kids how trusting Jesus brought you peace. Read one chapter at a time to let them process slowly, and close each time with a prayer for courage and hope in God's plan.

Discussion Questions

1. **After Chapter 1 (Paradise or Hades):**
   "What do you think paradise feels like? How does knowing Jesus is there make death less scary?"

2. **After Chapter 2 (Second Coming):**
   "Imagine getting a new, forever body like Emma's. What would you love to do with it?"

3. **After Chapter 3 (Millennial Reign):**
   "What would a peaceful world with Jesus look like? How can we live out His love right now?"

4. **After Chapter 4 (Satan's Defeat):**
   "Why do you think God wins over evil? How does that

give you hope for the future?"

5. **After Chapter 5 (Great White Throne):**
   "What does it mean to trust Jesus for eternal life? How can we share that hope with others?"

Final Encouragement

You don't need to be a Bible expert to guide your kids. Emma's story, paired with God's Word, is your roadmap. Let their questions lead the way, and trust Jesus to light the path for your family's journey toward hope.

10

About the Author

Christian A. Dickinson is an educator, author, and mentor passionate about helping readers explore God's truth with clarity and creativity. With more than 20 years of experience as a teacher, principal, and coach across private, public, and virtual schools, Christian brings a unique blend of leadership, faith, and insight to his writing.

He has authored more than ten Bible commentary books and devotional series for athletes, guiding readers to understand Scripture, grow in faith, and apply God's wisdom in daily life. Christian's work combines personal reflection, theological insight, and practical guidance, helping readers of all ages navigate life's questions with hope, courage, and purpose.

Christian lives in Tallahassee, Florida, with his wife, Morgan, and their children. Together, they are dedicated to nurturing faith, character, and curiosity in their family, students, and community through teaching, mentoring, and faith-based educational programs.

11

More Books by Christian A. Dickinson

I f you enjoyed *Beyond Heaven*, you may also appreciate these Christ-centered resources:

Reengineering Eden: God's Loving Plan to Restore Creation

From Eden's fall to a radiant new creation, God's love reengineers a broken world. Christian A. Dickinson traces this divine design—through Babel's scattering, Israel's calling, Naaman's faith, Christ's living water, and Pentecost's unity—offering a hope that anchors 2025's tech-driven challenges. Blending vivid scripture, personal reflection, and a heart for his children and grandchildren, this book unveils how every fracture becomes a foundation for restoration. With insights on AI's modern "towers" and invitations to live God's plan, *Reengineering Eden* guides believers to trust the Designer who turns chaos into communion. Perfect for seekers, families, and those longing for eternal purpose.

Reengineering Eden: Behind the Veil of Eden

See the Bible like its first readers did. *Reengineering Eden shows the plan. Reengineering Eden: Behind the Veil of Eden* shows the players—God's divine council, rebellious giants, and Jesus' triumph.Christian A. Dickinson guides students through the Bible's unseen world, unpacking Psalm 82, Genesis 6, Babel, and the Cross with vivid stories and study helps. Discover why Jesus faced the "gates of Hades" and your role in God's cosmic victory to restore Eden.

The Curse of Time: Time Began When Eternity Broke
A theological and personal exploration of time as a consequence of sin—not a neutral part of creation. Drawing from Scripture, Church Fathers, and moments of divine encounter, this book challenges the assumption that time was God's original design and invites readers to rediscover the eternal now of God's presence.

Roar of 'Ēzer: Reclaiming God's Vision for Women's Strength
From Eden's garden to the early church, God named women *'ēzer*—rescuer, strength-bearer, equal partner in His image. This compelling biblical exploration invites women to rise, not as shadows but as co-laborers in God's kingdom. With Scripture, story, and a call to courage, *Roar of 'Ēzer* reveals that women were never meant to shrink. They were always meant to roar.

The Unseen Pattern: God's Rhythms in Time, Beauty, and the Gospel

From sunrises to spirals, suffering to celebration, God weaves His redemptive rhythm through creation and Scripture. Christian A. Dickinson, with a mentor's heart and a mathematician's eye, unveils these patterns in stories of loss, hope, and worship, guiding readers to the cross where every moment finds meaning. Blending personal reflection, biblical insight, and invitations to pause, this devotional invites you to notice God's design, trust His grace, and live the harmony of His Gospel.

Jesus Was Funnier Than You Think: Unlocking His Wit, Wisdom, and Unexpected Humor

A fresh look at the wit and humor of Jesus Christ — revealing the brilliant, joyful ways He taught truth and disarmed pride.

Every Tear Remembered: God's Presence in Our Grief

A reflection on sorrow, healing, and hope through the lens of God's enduring love.

The Prophetic Equation: Thirty Prophets. One Christ. Zero Coincidence.

An exploration of how thirty prophetic voices across centuries, kingdoms, and crises converge with stunning precision in Jesus Christ — revealing that Scripture is not random, but a masterpiece of divine design.

Micah 6:8: A Prophetic Bridge to Jesus

A concise biblical commentary exploring how one ancient verse points forward to the life and ministry of Christ.

It's All or Nothing: How Jesus Raised the Standard from Tithing to Full Surrender

A biblical commentary challenging traditional views of tithing by exploring Jesus' call to radical, Spirit-led generosity.

FULL CIRCLE: PREGAME — A Devotional Series for Athletes

Before the whistle blows and the lights come up, PREGAME challenges athletes to prepare their hearts as well as their bodies. With powerful stories, Scripture reflections, and real talk from the locker room, Coach Dickinson and Anthony "Diso" Paradiso equip competitors to lead with faith, play with integrity, and honor Christ in every moment.